FLAVORTOWN

ALSO BY DANNY CAINE

How to Resist Amazon and Why (Microcosm Publishing)

El Dorado Freddy's (w/ Tara Wray, Belt Publishing)

Continental Breakfast (Mason Jar Press)

FLAVORTOWN
DANNY CAINE
POEMS

HB

First Edition, 2021
ISBN 978-0-578-87634-4

Edited by Gabrielle Lawrence
Cover and interior layout by Peter Barnfather

Cover photograph by Tara Wray
Flavortown map design by Kevin Cannon

Type set in Bergamo Pro, FontSite Inc.

Printed in the United States of America

Published by Harpoon Books
harpoonreviewbooks.com

for Kara

CONTENTS

NOTHING TO DO HERE

THE WIENERMOBILE SONNETS

THE AMERICAN KIDWEST

NOTHING TO DO HERE

———

"On camera, I once said, 'this pizza looks like a manhole cover in Flavortown.' Willy Wonka had a chocolate stream, you know? […] It's like one of those things in The Matrix: You can only get down with Flavortown if you believe in Flavortown. I have people walk up to me and say, 'Hey, I'm a citizen of Flavortown.' I have people that want to pledge to be a city council member of Flavortown or the mechanic. It doesn't stop. What would be the airline of Flavortown? Sausage Airlines?"

— Guy Fieri

GUY FIERI TALKS TO HIMSELF IN HIS TRAILER'S MIRROR BEFORE GOING ON SET

> Hittin #stagecoach2019 with a case of
> #SantoMezquila with my boy @HunterFieri
> #realdeal #smokehouse #unicorn
> — @GuyFieri · 11:14 PM · Apr 25, 2019

You're the realdeal smokehouse unicorn.
You're a dry rubbed medium-rare specimen.
You butcher, you host, you love, you taste.
You tableside throwdown, you locally sourced
can of whoopass, you USDA certified lover,
you fiery red Camaro, you hole in the wall.
You're a guy's Guy, a chef's chef, a mogul's mogul
and a ladies' man. Pop culture's jalapeno popper.
You have an intellect that's smoked low and slow.
May you rise up on the wings of a Buffalo.
Get out there and do it, you magnificent bleached
bastard. Do it for Flavortown. Do it for the dead.
Do it for your boy. Do it for the people
who can't stop laughing at you.

YOU CAN TAKE THE KID OUT OF THE MIDWEST

Sure, we're eating oysters now—
me, hot sauce, she, mignonette—
but at least we're talking
about coming from buffet families.

You never forget your Ponderosa plate:
Me, drumsticks and blue Jello. Yellow
if they didn't have blue. She, a pile
of ham cubes drowning in ranch dressing.

WHERE EXACTLY IS FLAVORTOWN, USA?

with help from shitguyfierisays.tumblr.com

Like a manhole cover in Flavortown. Like
a speed bump in Flavortown. Like a hot-dog
lasso on the ranch in Flavortown. Like a giant
Play-Doh machine in Flavortown. Like a blackjack
dealer at the Flavortown casino. Like a hot tub
in Flavortown. I want to be the mayor
of Flavortown. A conductor on the train
going to Flavortown. The driver on the bus
going to Flavortown. A big hamburger might
be the steering wheel on the bus that's going
to Flavortown. That's in the tank that fuels the bus
that's going to Flavortown. Hitting the road
in search of Flavortown has been quite a trip.
Four or five bites into this and I'm pulling in
to the depot of Flavortown. You can find that
dictionary in the Flavortown library. What would
be the airline of Flavortown? Sausage Airlines?
The first discovered culinary cave of Flavortown.
A lightning bolt of an idea in Flavortown. Mining
for food in Flavortown river. I feel like I'm gonna
have surgery here at Flavortown memorial. I'm
a citizen of Flavortown, a city council member
of Flavortown. Of course, there's no Flavortown—
unless you believe in it.

IT'S A DOMINO'S CHRISTMAS

"Even gas station food can save you."
    – Louise Erdrich, *Future Home of the Living God*

When Cleveland pitcher Carlos Carrasco
first came to the states, he ate Domino's
dine-in for 90 days straight. I can't think
of anything I've done for 90 days in a row
but I can tell you how to get to
the Effingham Fairfield Inn from
the exit and that's not as easy as
it should be. That we have to stop
for gas in Terre Haute where they sell
jerky in sheets, and in Ashland where
there's a taco bell and a Christian gift shop
both inside the truck stop. That Grandma
trips always have soundtracks: driving to
Columbus we listen to Springsteen
in 1978 at the Cleveland Agora.
Driving back it's the *Santaland Diaries*.
Driving to Roanoke we try to remember
what your dad said was the fastest
way. That the Jello has canned
pineapple floating in it like flakes
in a lime green snow globe.
I don't make the rules I just say them
out loud, mumbled like Hanukkah

blessings from the transliterations.
I don't know why the menorah rests
atop a single sheet of tin foil atop
the stove, but it's not my job to ask
questions. It's my job to pass out
presents, but only if I'm wearing
the same scratchy Santa hat. I don't
know where it came from—maybe
a January Walgreens—but I do
know I've never seen a family
VHS tape without it. What is
Christmas anyway if not the same
shit in a different year, thank God.

WELCOME TO FLAVORTOWN

"That one sandwich is all you need.
You can tear up the rest of the menu."
– Guy Fieri

This is what you need to know:
all of our restaurants (sorry, joints)
have been on TV at least once
and there's a little Food Network icon
next to the items you're supposed
to order. Often, they're in bold type
or a different color or a gray box.
It makes things easier. I don't know
why they even list the other stuff.

S10E01: DRESSEL'S PUBLIC HOUSE, ST. LOUIS

INT Hallway outside the bathroom at Dressel's Public House. POET waits for the one-stall bathroom to become available. He stares at a poster of Guy Fieri that says GUY WAS HERE. It is signed.

> POET (v.o.)
> I feel like maybe I've seen this episode?

A clip plays. INT Kitchen, Dressel's Public House. GUY FIERI bites into a large sandwich.

> GUY
> That would be a triple d hall of fame sandwich. Out. Standing. Out of bounds. Off the hook. Shut the front door. Call a neighbor and get a ticket.

INT Dressel's Public House Dining Room. POET sits at a table with THE PEOPLE FROM THE MEETING. He eats the same sandwich from the previous clip.

> POET
> Mmmmmmmmm.

> POET (v.o.)
> What choice did I have? I ordered the sandwich. It was pretty good. Maybe not out-of-bounds-off-the-hook good, but good. Heidi's Fish and Chips over there looks a lot better.

IT'S A CRACKER BARREL CHRISTMAS

Try *enter* through the gift shop,
passing four themed trees before
you get to the kids who take
your name. According to
their aprons, they are rising stars.
The roving employees, fully
risen, have empty baskets and
I don't know why. On the
fourth day of Christmas,
Cracker Barrel gave to me
a measuring spoon set, each
shaped like a pine, each labeled:
¼ tsp of LOVE. ½ tsp of PEACE.
1 tsp of JOY, 1 tbsp of BELIEVE
because that much of anything
needs to be a verb. Believe it
when I tell you Ray and Wilma
Yoder just finished their quest
to visit every Cracker Barrel
in America. I used to want
to go to every ballpark but
now Ray and Wilma gave me
another idea. We would like
to welcome DANNY PARTY
OF TWO to Cracker Barrel:
your table is ready! I used to

hate that my parents went to
Applebee's and Target on
Friday nights, now here I am
at Cracker Barrel on the way
to Ikea. At what point do these
places stop being ironic things
to write about and just become
what I like? Cracker Barrel
courtesy announcement for
DANNY PARTY OF ONE:
that point is already
Christmas passed.

THE FLAVORTOWN CITIZENSHIP TEST, WITH ONE TRICK QUESTION

What is the difference between a diner,
a drive-in, and a dive? How much bacon
is appropriate to put on a burger? Name
three foods that require a stick when
deep fried. On a fourth down in a game
his team would ultimately win, Eagles
backup quarterback Nick Foles becomes
the first QB to make a touchdown reception
in Super Bowl history. As you watch, do you
dip your wings in ranch or bleu cheese?
What is the difference between comfort food
and home cookin'? Write out the lyrics
to "Cheeseburger in Paradise," the Flavortown
National Anthem. What does it mean when
a server calls you "sweetie"? What does it mean
when a server calls you "hon"? Which crime
carries the longest sentence: A. Boiling ribs.
B. Charging for chips and salsa. C. Making
your own ketchup in-house. Or D. Brunch.
Name three dishes that do NOT benefit
from the addition of pulled pork. That
was the trick question.

GUY FIERI IMAGINES INVITING PETE WELLS TO FLAVORTOWN

> Mr. Fieri did not say why he was closing the
> restaurant, which features what he calls "American
> comfort food gone wild." The demise could not be
> attributed to the scathing, no-stars review by Pete
> Wells of *The New York Times* because that appeared
> back in November 2012, shortly after the restaurant
> opened. The review, which went viral, noted,
> among other details, "how very far from awesome
> the Awesome Pretzel Chicken Tenders are."
> – *New York Times*

Your mayor was photographed
eating pizza
with a fork.

Hamilton played here too—
tickets were only $8 and everybody
who wanted one got one.

Let me book you
a first class flight
on Sausage Airlines.

Roll your eyes all you want, Pete,
but remember how many people only know
your name because you tried to shit on mine.

ALL I WANT FOR CHRISTMAS
IS ALL I WANT FOR CHRISTMAS IS YOU

The closest
any of us will ever get
to the Rockefeller Center rink
is listening to this
at skull crushing volume.
It's every Linus and Lucy
dance at the same time
in double time.
The city I live in doesn't
even have an escalator
but I can still turn on
any radio to any station
and step into a snow globe.
I know Mariah won't save us
but when the intro turns
into piano turns into drums
turns into verse every time
I think she might.

TILT-SHIFT TOWN

It's not just small,
it's a tilt-shift town,
everything blurry
around the edges.
There's nothing
to do except sit
outside the Dari King
(we don't even get
the real thing)
and wait for the train
to rumble by.
When the Subway
(not a train,
a sandwich shop)
opened there were
lines out the door.
Someday let a hand
descend from the sky
and move me
somewhere else.

CAMPAIGN ROBOCALLS IN FLAVORTOWN

He isn't right for Flavortown. He eats
his pizza with a knife and fork. He thinks
Taco Bell is America's best Mexican food.
He eats his hot dogs with ketchup. He eats
his hot dogs without ketchup. He makes
guacamole with peas in it. He was filmed
biting into a tamale before unwrapping it.
He eats cheesesteaks with Swiss cheese
instead of Cheez Wiz. His favorite flavor
of chips is reduced sodium. He's never
had paella or crawfish or real ramen. He's
elitist, out of touch, thinks arugula prices
are too high, thinks a way to save our farms
is to grow more Belgian Endive. Vote
carefully on Tuesday; we wouldn't want
to elect someone who isn't authentic.

IT'S A TEXAS ROADHOUSE CHRISTMAS

Last weekend, zombies walked
the streets, and today Texas Roadhouse
has its trees up. Peanut shells crack like
ice under my feet. Limit one kicker tube
per margarita. The first Texas Roadhouse
was in Indiana. The stuffed ram has two
full sets of antlers, one fuzzy with bells.
On the country veg plate can one of my choices
be a single chicken finger? An upcharge is fine.
The waiter visits three times before
the drinks arrive. He calls Kara "hon'"
like a person who has learned to do so
from a training video. The music is country
2009 but it might as well be Christmas.
This place makes me miss
a place I'm not from
that might not even exist.

ROMANCE IS IN THE AIR

Romance is in the air.
And in this cup.
Taste for yourself...
– @DairyQueen · 6:30 PM · Jan 29, 2019

How we decided on a date eating Dairy Queen
in the park behind the high school
I don't remember. I do remember bag boys
were supposed to ask cashiers on dates, so I did.
It took forever to find Anna's house in the labyrinth
of her subdivision. Smith Dr., Smith Ct.,Smith St..
She lived on one of them. Maybe the ad I saw
for the DQ Chicken Finger box was the hunger
GPS guiding me to the drive-through and then
the park. Or, every date that summer was eating
fast food in a park behind a school. I do remember
this: Anna ate a dipped cone but finished it in the car
before we got to the park. She wasn't impressed
with me and I don't blame her. I do remember:
I opened that cardboard box of food and realized,
holy shit, everything in there—
fries, Texas Toast, tenders—
was the same color.

AN OFF NIGHT IN FLAVORTOWN

"Don't waste your time on a frozen pizza."
  – Guy Fieri

Man I don't feel like going out tonight
but we can't eat cereal for dinner.
We can't eat plain old grilled cheese for dinner.
We can't eat leftovers for dinner.
We can't eat bologna sandwiches for dinner.
We can't eat scrambled eggs for dinner.
We can't eat whatever's in the fridge
for dinner. We can't eat Ortega powder tacos
for dinner since they outlawed that stuff.
Same goes for Stouffer's frozen French Bread Pizza.
We certainly can't eat *salads* for dinner.
This mole won't be ready until Tuesday and the brisket
needs 12 more hours in the smoker. Why don't I just
run to the gas station and get some prime rib to go?

SOMETHING ELSE AT JIMMY JOHN'S

Today turned montage
walking down Mass Street
all music and sun and breeze
and smiling people in good
clothes. I thought *you must
change your life* so I ordered
something else from
Jimmy John's. I don't
recommend it. Your
usual is your usual
for a reason, no matter
what song is playing
in your head as you amble
through a day aching
with sunlight.

IT'S A WAFFLE HOUSE CHRISTMAS

The hotel closest to Grandma's
closest to affordable doesn't have
breakfast but it does share
a parking lot with a Waffle House.
So Christmas morning, over
the curbs and through the
gas station hedge to Waffle's
House we go. As soon as
the door chimes we feel it—
Tiny Tim doesn't show us
to our table but he might
as well. All the seats are full
except for ours and the waitress
is in a good mood. The cook isn't
on a 45-minute smoke break
and all our food comes hot
at once and people are
laughing and cheerful, but
they're not singing or anything
thank god
and the whole place feels—
what's the word—clean?
It's a Christmas miracle,
a Waffle House that looks
the way Waffle House
looks like in your sepia

memories. It's enough
to make me want to stand
on a table, spread my arms
and yell

"God bless us,
    every scattered,
    smothered, and
    covered one of us."

THE FLAVORTOWN AMBASSADOR

You ambassador in a Camaro—
no border wall can stop you
because there are no border walls
in Flavortown. The car runs on gas,
the passengers run on pork belly
and jalapenos, chili powder and brisket.
When you're in a convertible this fast
with a stomach this full, you shrink
the world. Mexico in Oakland.
Nepal in Columbus. Italy in Lansing.
It doesn't matter where you rest
your sunglasses. It doesn't matter
if you get sauce in your goatee.
Just tell us where to go and what to order.

S09E19: STANDARD DINER, ALBUQUERQUE

INT Standard Diner. A self-consciously hip update to the "classic diner" look. POET sits at a table with CONFERENCE FRIENDS. They chat and eat.

> POET (v.o.)
> I didn't want meatloaf, even if there was a little clipart Guy next to it on the menu. My food is pretty standard, but everyone else seems to be really loving their meatloaf.

FLAVORTOWN GOSSIP

Calling him a guy is like calling The Boss a boss—
yes, but there's so much more. I heard he's a Republican.
I heard it's a wig. I heard he's gonna run for mayor.
I heard he paid for the statue himself. I heard he doesn't
even pick the restaurants for Triple D. But did you hear
he's kind of a jerk on-set? No way, he's a saint. After all
the dude spends his life giving small businesses free
publicity. I've had Donkey Sauce and it's delicious.
I heard he didn't leave his house for days after the
New York Times review went online. He's a people pleaser.
All he wants is to be liked. He rolls with the jokes, leans in
to the persona, but all he wants is acceptance. And ribs.
We shouldn't psychoanalyze. We're not his therapists.
Sure. But know what? His therapist is in my book club.

S09E10: WOODYARD BBQ, KANSAS CITY

"...they might mean more to one
another than even they realize."
– Thrillist.com on Guy Fieri
and Anthony Bourdain

There are two types of people:
Guy Fieris and Anthony Bourdains.
They do not get along.

TONY
[Guy Fieri is] like if Ed Hardy fucked a Juggalo.

GUY
I don't like him making fun of people, and I don't like him
talking shit. And he's never talked shit to my face.

TONY
Guy Fieri kind of looks like he's been designed by committee.

GUY
You have nothing else to fucking worry about than if I have
bleached hair or not? I mean, fuck.

TONY
If you can't tell jokes about Guy Fieri, comedy as we know
it is dead.

GUY
I know he's definitely gotta have issues.

Anthony Bourdain died on June 8, 2018. Among the many things he spoke about with clarity and intelligence was his past substance abuse. It's hard to think that any part of the previous two sentences has anything to do with Guy Fieri, but here they are in a poem together, and here Guy is on TV (All. The. Time.) when I'd trade the entire run of *Guy's Grocery Games* for just one more episode of *Parts Unknown*.

Guy Fieri's courtside selfie with Ludacris
at the 2019 All Star Game has nothing to do
with Anthony Bourdain's death. Right?

Does it change things if my entire family used to sit down together, happily, to watch *Triple D?* I can say TV isn't important, but my brother and I are now grown. I live in Kansas and they all live in Ohio and the moments where we're all happy on the couch are now rare.

Does it change things if I spent many early morning hours watching *Parts Unknown* on a quiet laptop while comforting my newborn son, who was very bad at sleeping? That he was born close enough to Tony's death that the two events will always be linked in my mind? That someone I've never met can leave a sudden and surprising chasm of grief, that the timing of all this joy and grief left me as wide-awake and restless as the baby in my arms?

No matter how much I watch
them on TV, how much do I really
know about these men?

GUY

If you get thrown off by the fact that I have bleach-blondehair and tattoos, and listen to rock and roll, […] then you really don't know me well enough to […] be making an opinion about me. But that's fine.

A Google image search reveals only a few pictures of Anthony Bourdain and Guy Fieri together. In one, they appear to be on stage together at some kind of food show. Guy is grinning. Tony is taller. Guy's in a Bulls jersey and chains, wraparound shades. Tony's in a blue oxford. Guy holds a microphone pointed at his own face. Tony has his index finger pointed at Guy's chest. Tony looks angry. The few other photos I could find are group shots with multiple celebrity chefs. Tony and Guy are always separated by at least one person. I don't think this thing was just an act for TV.

TONY

I look at Guy Fieri and I just think, 'Jesus, I'm glad that's not me.'

GUY

I like my haircut the way it is.

Of course I like to think I'm a Tony.
It's hard to imagine wanting to be a Guy. But I suspect
there's no sorting hat, that it's a spectrum.

Maybe it's a question of place. Places. A short but mostly representative list of places Anthony Bourdain has been filmed eating: Copenhagen. Tokyo. New York City. Paris. Greece. Myanmar. Los Angeles. Peru. Detroit. Mexico City. Lyon. Cuba. Buenos Aires. He's been filmed eating at Waffle House, but he's also been filmed eating at Noma.

A short but mostly representative list of places Guy Fieri has been filmed eating: Wichita. West Lafayette. Flagstaff. Omaha. Boise. Sacramento. Reno. Lackawanna. Duluth. Spokane. Tampa. Carmel, Indiana. Roy, Utah. As far as I can tell, there are no pictures of Guy Fieri in a tie.

> Maybe a heartland/coastal thing
> is too easy, but can you imagine
> Guy in Ethiopia? Tony in Topeka?

It's surprisingly hard to find out which places both men have been filmed eating at. Documentation of *Triple D* online is amazingly thorough, with a comprehensive Wikipedia page and several fan-run databases outlining the restaurants (sorry, joints) Guy has featured. You can click on a map. There's not as much of this for *No Reservations* and *Parts Unknown*, in part because Tony seemed to resist making a pure "go here and eat this" kind of show. Especially later in the run of *Parts Unknown*, Tony ate at homes and backyards more often than restaurants. It makes for good storytelling. Still, kind of a bummer to watch a meal I can never eat in beautiful HD cinematography.

> Sometimes I just want
> to be told where to go
> and what to order.

They've both done whole episodes about Kansas City. They've both been filmed eating at Woodyard Barbeque (Andrew Zimmern was filmed eating there too, and according to a van in the parking lot, Nigella Lawson?).

GUY

We're going to the source, a place a lot of Kansas City BBQ joints get their wood from [...] 5 years ago, owner Frank Schloegel decided if the wood's good enough for everybody else he'd start cookin on it too, and add BBQ to the business.

TONY

First and foremost a wood yard that provided fuel to Kansas City pitmasters, they decided they might as well get in the game themselves.

Guy got there first, filming on April 12, 2010 for an episode of *Triple D* that first aired two months later. I can't figure out when Tony visited, but the episode of *No Reservations* aired April 16, 2012. Guy did the same thing he does at every restaurant: he watched the chef prepare the signature dish, often combining small bowls of spices into larger bowls. Then, Guy ate the dish and made effusive noises and declarations.

GUY

Is that turmeric? I'm in Kansas City, right? Cardamom, seriously? That is one of the most peculiar rubs I've ever seen. Cardamom, turmeric, and cloves? In Kansas City? On Pork ribs? No sugar? Alright [...] Mmmmm. Woah. Those ribs are knockout. Tons of flavor.

In his segment, Tony barely mentioned the food.

TONY

My ribs and brisket were delicious.

Does it change things if I say the ribs are perhaps the worst I've ever eaten in Kansas City? Will you believe me more than the TV men? The ribs are bland and tough, and I assure you that, at least when I went, they were neither "delicious" nor "knockout".

So what interested Guy Fieri and Anthony Bourdain (and Andrew Zimmern and Nigella Lawson, too, if the van is to be believed) about this place that can't even make the real KC top twenty? It has to be the look: Woodyard Bar-B-Que is wearing a great "authentic KC BBQ joint" costume, with its outdoor-only seating, its rickety building, and its muddy parking lot out back. It's what people want to see when they watch KC BBQ joints on TV.

Instead of a discussion of the food or any of these issues surrounding it, Tony threw his show's narrative energy into one of those *No Reservations* gags. You remember them: high concept skits and bits. Tony mostly got rid of them for *Parts Unknown*. In the case in question, the Akron rock band the Black Keys "kidnaps" Tony and "takes him" to Woodyard Bar-B-Que.

The Guy Fieri effect is well-documented in boosting featured restaurants' bottom lines. People tend to advertise having been on Triple D, even years after the fact, since these shows will air in reruns until the earth stops spinning. On their way into the joint, Tony and the Black Keys surely walked past Woodyard's myriad handmade signs. One of the signs was a souvenir of the day Guy filmed there. In spray-painted scrawl it says "WOODYARD BAR-B-QUE TODAY MONDAY APRIL 12 DINERS DRIVE-INS AND DIVES ARE COMING "YO" GUY." This must be why Tony and the Black Keys found themselves on camera making fun of Guy Fieri with no apparent provocation.

DAN AUERBACH

What's one of your Guy Fieri jokes?

TONY

Oh, I mean, it's just so easy, you know?

PATRICK CARNEY

Every single episode it's the same thing. He's always eating giant burritos and he's always like "Bitchin burrito, bro. Oh, the sweet, then the heat, ohhh man."

TONY

Gotta do the faux gang sign.

More screen time was devoted to making fun of Guy Fieri than the food itself, and there is no introduction, segue, or context for the jokes except for the fact that everywhere Tony appeared in 2012, he was ready to be filmed making fun of Guy Fieri. But that needs no context. Like Nickelback, you don't need a reason to make fun of Guy Fieri.

UNNAMED INTERVIEWER

When's the last time you remember just laughing until you cried? Just, like, screaming, laughing?

TONY

Guy Fieri's tweet that he was on the way to a Nickelback concert. It was the funniest fuckin' thing! I was like, of course!

STAND-UP COMIC SHANE TORRES

Can someone please explain to me what the hell Guy Fieri ever did to anyone?…because he has flames on his shirt, everyone shits all over this dude like he's a member of Nickelback. And by the way, what the hell did Nickelback ever do?

> As much as I love Tony, has Guy
> ever used his platform
> to make fun of somebody?

GUY

I'm not super flamboyant about expressing [my opinion] about other people.

Guy Fieri issued no statement or Tweet or anything about Tony's death. Far be it from me to criticize the silence, as I try to avoid performative online grief for celebrity death. Instead, I tend to wait months or years and then write very long poems, but even I tweeted something about how Tony's death wrecked me. Guy's tweets immediately before and after the announcement of Bourdain's suicide are unrelated, banal. I don't know what Tony would have wanted and I don't know why Guy stayed silent, because I still don't know anything about either of these men, only that I recognize parts of myself in both of them.

TONY

You know what, it's Guy's world… I'm just living in it.

THE WIENERMOBILE SONNETS

———

"All my happiest moments seem
to revolve around meat in tube form."
– Anthony Bourdain

"That's a righteous dog, dude."
– Guy Fieri

THE NOSTALGIC WIENERMOBILE

I don't have a picture of my dad
next to the Wienermobile but I remember
we saw it together. A Boy Scout trip
to the Henry Ford museum? A parade?
Maybe just the parking lot at Giant Eagle?
The Grand Prix where I tried to order a hotdog
but got an Italian sausage so spicy it made me
cry? I don't even have these memories—
I have memories of my dad telling me
those memories. Here's what I do remember:
the line at the Oscar Meyer career fair booth
was shorter than all the other ones. Everyone
wanted to talk to Google. I remember everyone
at Oscar Meyer had a thing with handshakes.

WHY DO YOU WANT TO BE A HOTDOGGER?

after Dave Ihlenfeld

Because I have a thing for grocery
store parking lots and gas stations.
Because I've never eaten enough
hot dogs. Because it was my only
second interview. Because
my parents' generation destroyed
the job market. Because Oscar Mayer
will give me health insurance. Because
I look good in red. Because I still
believe in the myth of the open road.
Because it's the adventure of a lifetime.
Because I want to believe that every exit
is actually different from the next. Because
who the fuck knows *what I truly want to be?*

THE HOTDOGGER'S FATHER

Is that what you want to be? He roared.
A truck driver? Only $21,000 a year? Do they
give you health insurance? Do they feed you something
other than hot dogs? You don't even get hot dogs?
I told him room and board is included.
You better get used to shitty hotel breakfasts. Why
don't you just go to grad school? At least that lasts
more than a year. Every time we talked for months
it was tuned too sharp. But you should have
seen him when I pulled into his driveway in that
beautiful machine. You should see the photo
of us standing in front of it. You should've
heard him when he told me to tell my bosses—
any crews driving through here, they eat dinner at my house.

THE HOTDOGGER'S WISH

Oh I wish that I could drive through at McDonald's
or Wendy's or Arby's or pull into any old car wash
or park in a garage. That laundry wasn't an ordeal.
Oh I wish that I could see out my back window,
that I had a back window at all, that I didn't have to
overthink every right turn. That I could wear whatever
shirt I wanted to. That I could call a full size box of cereal
"mine." That I could sleep in the same bed for more than
two nights in a row. That I could pull into any parking spot
and know I'll fit. That a stranger could approach me
without asking me for something. That a stranger could
approach me and ask me for something other than
a weenie whistle. That I could drive somewhere in a Civic
or Camry. That I could drive anywhere without being so seen.

TAKE A PICTURE OF THE HOT DOG, NOT THE HOT DOGGER

In my childhood home videos I love being seen—
outside the frame of my brother I shout
"take a picture of me!" I could say the same now
every time I see someone do that head nudge to get
me out of their shot. Sorry, the Hotdogger manual
dictates that we put the Whistle Table *right here*.
Just try to ignore little old me, The Guy To Whom
The Family Gives The Phone Before Lining Up.
I know all the camera apps, I'm good, I take a bunch.
But just once I'm gonna switch it to selfie, just once
I'm gonna take a video instead: 15 seconds of a family
trying to smile and keep their eyes open in the sun.
By the time they realize what happened, we'll be
laughing, too far away for them to catch up.

THE HOTDOGGER FALLS IN LOVE

Ketchup Kelly turns her turn signal on
too soon. She leaves the Wienermobile
interior, to be honest, a bit messy.
She can't play the jingle on the whistle
so she makes me do it. I'm sick of her
Ariana Grande. She always orders
the Filet-O-Fish and it's starting to smell
like tartar sauce in here. She never gets
the table out from the back. She always
says she's too tired—*can you take*
this shift? Still, when our rooms
in some heartland Fairfield Inn are
next to each other and I can hear her
on the phone with her boyfriend, I can't sleep.

THE HOTDOGGER'S BAD NIGHT

I can never sleep this far from home
and I've already seen this episode of Triple D.
Breakfast doesn't start for four more hours
and each of these pillows is mostly lump.
On my phone I look at my friends at concerts,
my friends at weddings I wasn't invited to.
I don't think a single business in this town
is even open, not even the gas station
across the pond between here
and the Cracker Barrel (also closed).
They've even turned off the fountain.
I only have one outfit that isn't red and yellow.
I put it on and walk into the Amarillo night, just
another creep in a parking lot.

THE AFTERNOON DESK CLERK
MEETS THE HOTDOGGERS

Gingerly it creeps into the parking lot.
It stops as if wondering whether it can
fit under the porte cochère. It can. That's
a thing people don't know about my job.
Most trucks can fit under your average Holiday Inn
Express porte cochère. Another thing people
don't know—it's called a porte cochère.
The door hisses open. Our parking lot
is almost always empty, but now people with phones
are out there taking pictures. One more thing
people don't know: I get so sick of looking at Civics,
at Midwestern children and cheap suitcases. But
here are these two in scarlet windbreakers
handing me a whistle. It's a good day.

THE HOTDOGGER'S PARADE

Today is a good day, like an Instagram Filter
for the whole world that makes everyone
look tan. No parking lot. Instead, a parade.
We're between the marching band
and the mayoral candidates. Children
smile and reach their fingers towards us
grasping at whistles. Our wake is a cloud
of plastic squeals. I've stopped really seeing
the truck, but today, I see people see it
for the first time, or the first time
in a long time—and now it's more
than a dumb job while I figure out what to do
after college. A bit. It's not like I'm about to go eat
a hot dog, but maybe the parking lots aren't so bad.

THE HOTDOGGER'S PARKING LOT

Some supermarket parking lots are better
than others. Some shine like Kelly today—
making children laugh and parents mouth
silent thanks as they head back to their minivans.
What are road friends when the road ends?
Kelly got a call today that her top choice
masters program accepted her. We've got
9 weeks left but I can't help thinking of
last times—could this be our last QuikTrip?
Our last parade? Our last marriage proposal
to record and send to the corporate Twitter?
If people were more interested in parking lots
this year would make a good book. Maybe I can
get something out of it. An essay. Or a sonnet.

THE HOTDOGGER'S SONNET

Joey Baloney says it's like a sonnet,
the perfect Wienermobile visit. A pun
in the first line, a smile in the third.
In the fourth, we hand you a whistle
and in the sixth we show you
how to play the jingle. Then, a sticker
that says "I saw it." We beckon you
further into the poem—you climb
inside the Wienermobile and breathe
as you take it all in. Before you know it
we've hit the volta—you turn
to go somewhere else, into the grocery store
or another poem. Before you go, take
another picture. We'll be here all day.

THE HOTDOGGERS PUT
THE "OSCAR" IN OSCAR MEYER

We've been here all day doing nothing
but decking this thing out with balloons
and twinkle lights. My dad mailed me
his old tux. Corporate sent a bowtie
with hot dogs on it. When we saw "Oscars"
on the schedule, we could never imagine
it'd be this boring. It's the first time
we've ever been ignored, bypassed
by bystanders vying for a glimpse
of Gaga or Glenn Close. Laptop on dashboard,
we stream the show. We take a picture
for Twitter and pretend we're having fun.
It's a magic trick: drive to Hollywood,
make a 27-foot hot dog disappear.

THE HOTDOGGER'S ABSENCE

When a giant hot dog doesn't appear
around any corner, this town feels
different. Now every grocery store
parking lot is nothing but
a grocery store parking lot half full
of Accords and Altimas and fully
empty of any giant food, of any fun.
The weenie whistles have begun
their migration to junk drawers
or trash cans. Does he ever think
of the towns he's left as he drives
to the next town and the next?
No: every town he visits
is a town with a Wienermobile in it.

THE HOTDOGGER'S NEXT STEP

The Wienermobile is barely in the photo
of me and my dad a year ago in his driveway—
it's a red and yellow blur behind two guys smiling
for two different reasons. The smile I see when he
opens the door is the same one. Behind me
this time is not a Weinermobile, but a blue
Super Shuttle van headed to its next stop, bringing
only luggage and travelers, not joy and whistles.
I tell him *before you ask, I still don't know*
what's next. Ushering me in, he laughs.
What's next is dinner. Leave your bag here.
After the year you've had, I figured you'd be glad
to see some green veggies. I was so happy
to see that salad, I took a picture of it.

THE AMERICAN KIDWEST

———

"The minute that you become a father, certain truths
become immediately obvious to you. The first second you
see your daughter's head corkscrew out of the womb and open
her eyes, they are pretty much saying, 'Lose the Ramones shirt.'
So I've made some adjustments in my life… I sort of feel
in a heartfelt way for Guy [Fieri]. I wonder about him.
He's 52 years old and still rolling around in the flame outfit…
What does he do? How does Guy Fieri de-douche?"
– Anthony Bourdain

WHEN A BABY IS BORN IN FLAVORTOWN

Instead of "it's a boy!" or "it's a girl!"
they shout "red chile!" or "green chile!"
The little hats they put on their heads
at Flavortown Memorial have Harley
badges on them. Five percent of girls
born in Flavortown are named Harley.
The most popular name for guys is Guy.
There's a kegerator at each nurse's station.
They send you home with a bunch
of baby food purees. Flavors: fried chicken,
muffaletta, and sriracha. All the babies
in Flavortown love spice. All the parents
in Flavortown love their babies.
The babies sleep through the night
every night except two: Wrestlemania
and the Super Bowl. They can't
bear to miss it. The best restaurants
(sorry, joints) have baby shower registries.
Plus, if you remember to call them,
the second-best barbeque place
brings each set of new parents
a full rack of St. Louis Ribs.
The new parents really appreciate it.

THE BLUE MOON SUITE

> "…one of my personal early,
> early morning favorites, 'Blue Moon'."
> — Tom Waits as a Memphis Radio DJ
> in Jim Jarmusch's *Mystery Train*

I.

Today was Sam Brownback's last day
in office. He asked Kansans to fast
with him. I didn't. I ate frozen pizza

and sang you Elvis. Unborn, I like
the idea of singing to you so why not
start now? Research shows you can hear me,

recognize my voice. The only Elvis song
I have memorized is "Blue Christmas,"
but it's January. You surprise, you

person, you future child, I hope to never
have another blue blue blue Christmas
without you. You are the end of the world.

Later, I can't sleep so I go downstairs
to look at the moon—a supermoon eclipse
and somehow, a blue moon. I'd sing

that one to you if only I knew the words.
There's no way now to know
you'll be born on a full moon

and I will learn the words and I will
sing it to you every time you can't sleep,
which will be all the time.

2.

I didn't even want to have kids
        until I saw Alex singing
the nooks and crannies song
        to his daughter over Skype.
You've got lots of nooks and crannies
        it's time to clean them out.
Cleaning out your nooks and crannies
        that's what it's all about.
Her only movement
        during that diaper change
was the crawling
        of the grin across her face.
I don't know what kind of building
        Alex sleeps in when he's deployed.
Sometimes I imagine Quonset huts,
        sometimes yurts. Sometimes
tents where his fellow pilots
        can hear him singing.
I sleep in a house. I certainly
        can't fly a plane.
But I can sing and I guess
        I can be a dad.

3.

Is it okay to be pregnant at a concert?
When did midnight become too late
and why did it happen so fast?
Birthday Girl dances by herself
by the bathrooms and we watch, trying
to ignore the opener's tepid cover
of "Kiss." Waiting to be a dad is teaching me
all kinds of stuff. For example: no Prince cover
will ever be okay to me. I saw Guided by Voices
in this room. Too long, wrong lineup, but
I didn't have to think about bedtime or Kara's
sore back. I chose to leave early that night too
but leaving because you're tired and leaving
because you're old are two different things.

4.

The first step when we get to the hospital
is to pick out our baby. There's a pile
of babies on a table at the front. Do we want
a boy baby or a girl baby? Should the baby's
skin tone match ours? We still don't know
what we're having (we tell people
"a human" when they ask) so we opt for
dinosaur pajamas instead of blue or pink.
Only when we get to our seats do I realize
that our baby has some kind of tattoo—
it looks like an "n" above its temple.
The PowerPoint begins but all I can think
is that it's a bit early for tattoos. I love
our baby despite its questionable choices.

5.

I already love you, unborn child—
much more than this goddamned dresser
I'm building for your room. Had I known
the dresser came assembly required,
I would have ordered a different dresser.
Fear not, as my love for you is strong—
stronger than my love for part 3-AA
which the carpet seems to have swallowed.
I love you more than words can say,
and more than the fucking bag of screws
I somehow *lost*—without which
the drawers on the dresser in your room
will have no handles. The thought of you
carries me through my days and nights,
except for this one, as it's now midnight
and I still have to assemble the drawers
and find another allen wrench because
the one that came with the goddamn dresser
fucking broke—I didn't even know you could
break a fucking allen wrench, but like I said,
imminent fatherhood teaches you all kinds
of new things. My first lesson to you:
anything can be made shitty enough to break.
Your mother has left the room, tired
of my swearing and slamming things
to the ground. I don't slam things

to scare her or to irritate the neighbors.
I slam things because I love you, I can't wait
to hold you, to gently set you down
atop this dresser so I can change
your shitty diapers.

A CHILD'S FIRST WORDS IN FLAVORTOWN

As soon as he got teeth
I knew it was time
to give him
a Nashville Hot Chicken sandwich.
He took one bite, smiled,
and looked directly at me.
He said, I swear to god,
Whoa, that's off the hook—
and reader, it was.

THE AMERICAN KIDWEST

Grass swaddles the plains
like a swaddle. Our national anthem
is something off a children's album
from the library that puts babies to sleep
instantly—but only at extreme volume.
We eat at chain restaurants because
they have parking and car seat slings
and enough room to put them
next to the table. When our children
begin eating solid foods, there will be
something on those menus for them
to eat. Perhaps an illustrated cup
to take home. Our currency is snacks,
stuffed into diaper bags alongside
accessories and ephemera: Changing pads.
Thermometers. Extra keys. Outfits.
That gift certificate we lost months ago.
We strap mirrors to headrests.
We are known for our competence
and our freezers and our tired faces.
Our grocery stores are giant
and have parking spaces
for expectant and new mothers.
The carts warn us not to mount
our car seats onto the handles
but we do anyway. We know balance
and we'd catch our children
if they ever fell. They don't.

THREE VIEWS OF DILLONS

i. The Father's First Trip to Dillons

What the hell this Dillons doing,
carrying on? I had a son this week.
These people don't even know.
The cashier doesn't know. Overfriendly
produce guy doesn't know. Pajama shopper
doesn't know what Kara just did, just muscled
through. For now, I feel fine. It's my first
time out of the house alone and I got
a bit of sleep last night. Since everything
feels momentous, I pay attention
to the song on the PA: "Kiss," by Prince.
I love this song. My family is healthy
and I have $1.30 in fuel points.

2. *"Why is the Dillons So Lit RN?"*
   after a Video Seen on Facebook

Well the Dillons doesn't need a bar,
and the bar doesn't need a dude
strumming Dylan tunes during the 4:00
rush. The beer doesn't need to be $4,
or this good, and the Dillons bar doesn't
need to be well-lit and comfy. The man
doesn't need to play the song that takes me
right back to that one summer, and I
don't need to get up and start shaking
my hips. Bonnie and Charles and this woman—
a stranger!—don't need to join me. We don't
need to be dancing in a Dillons:
don't think twice, it's alright.

3. A Nickname for Every Dillons in Kansas,
   Starting with the Four in Lawrence

Dirty Dillons is a phenomenon and a concept.
Every town with multiple Dillons has one.
Inevitably, they are the best for reasons
that are hard to articulate.
– @ chancedibben · 1:35 PM · Dec 10, 2017

Dirty Dillons Fancy Dillons Regular Dillons Dapper Dillons
Diaper Dillons Dino Dillons Druggy Dillons Silly Dillons
SciFi Dillons Sexy Dillons Grocery Dillons Disco Dillons
Tee-Shirt Dillons Jesus Dillons Saucy Dillons Boujee Dillons
Dixie Dillons Tiki Dillons TV Dillons Chunky Dillons
Super Chunky Dillons Baby Dillons Bad Dillons Rabbit
Dillons Murder Dillons New Dillons Far Dillons The
Dillons Where Nobody Gives a Shit Oprah Dillons Fruit Fly
Dillons Starbucks Dillons Redneck Dillons Soulpatch
Dillons Pothole Dillons Democrat Dillons Walmart Dillons
Empty Dillons Turnpike Dillons Impulse Dillons Dimple
Dillons Viper Dillons Biker Dillons Busy Dillons Best
Dillons First Dillons Thirsty Dillons Turkey Dillons Sketchy
Dillons All Night Dillons Donut Dillons Country Dillons
Spring Break Dillons Fake Dillons Road Rage Dillons Dairy
Dillons Scary Dillons Mr. Dillons Taco Dillons Bizarro
Dillons Indoor Dillons Mini Dillons USA Dillons Kroger
Dillons Dillons Dillons

IN THE BAD WALMART'S PARKING LOT

Every town with two Walmarts
has a good one and a bad one.
Visiting cousin Jeff in New York,
I'm always impressed how he knows
which end of the train to get on,
and which door out of the station
is closest to where we're going.
That's cool, cousin Jeff, but
can you park by the right door
at Walmart based on your
shopping list, plus the likelihood
of any last-minute additions? *I* can.
The bad Walmart really is bad—
the Subway doesn't even have
Subway Smell, but sometimes
you need a Walmart that's as bad
as you feel. Sorry if that's melodramatic—
I'm writing this on my phone
in the bad Walmart parking lot
and the doors are so far away.

GOING TO THE DOCTOR IN FLAVORTOWN

He asks so I tell him.
I drink maybe sixty beers
per week but always
with the dudes and always
craft IPAs. He gives me
a fist bump before telling me
my cholesterol isn't high enough.

IT'S A HOLIDAY INN EXPRESS CHRISTMAS

Tell whoever says there's nothing
to do in Fremont, Indiana that
the Holiday Inn Express has
free cookies *all night*. I don't
remember what we were looking at
on the Business Center PC
stuck in New Year's Day snow
between Chicago and Cleveland,
but that's when we decided
to get married next New Year's Eve.
We should've been swimming
but neither of us ever remembers
to bring a suit. In a different
poem maybe we'd just swim in
our underwear like Bobby did
that one time, but I'm not Bobby
and I never will be. A lobby,
a tree, and Vince Guaraldi are
all we need for something to do
between now and when
we'll collapse into stiff sheets,
lumpy pillows, and each other.

PRETTY GOOD

I go to the bedroom to see if Kara's okay.
The baby's in the crib for the first time, feeling
pretty good, apparently. Tomorrow we'll try
to go to Target for the first time. I curl
around Kara. She says she feels pretty
good. I kiss her neck. *We need a new night*
light I say. *That feels pretty good* she says, and
also those fruit bars for the middle of the night.
Yes, I say. We're really making out now
but the doula said we have to wait
at least six weeks. Still, it feels pretty good.
We also need more newborn sized pants.
Yes. Yes we do, she sighs, and before we can
fall backwards to the bed we alert, silenced
by the sound of a cry from the nursery.

RIVALRY NIGHT IN FLAVORTOWN

The Flavortown Guys versus the dreaded
Cheddar Bay Biscuits. Our men look great.
They take a six point lead into halftime.
Beneath the bleachers, Flavortown girls
sit in Flavortown laps and part their lips
as Flavortown boys feed them chili dogs.
They are each other's napkins.

NORTHCOAST LOVESONG

to Adam & Rebecca, on the occasion of their wedding

they say you're having
a renaissance, that
there's new life in you,
they say you're the city
where you come from,
they say you're better
than Columbus, they say
you're on the rise you're
the hottest you're
the reason you're the
king you're back,
they say it's you
against the world,
they say there's no
mistake about it,
they say you two
are like the smile
+ Baker's face, like
the river + the jokes
about its burning,
bratwurst + perogies,
the St. Patrick's Day
parade + yelling
out a window

on Euclid,
like winter
+ complaining
about winter,
like road + salt,
like slush + streetlight,
like one cloud
of breath + another
cloud of breath,
like a head +
the shoulder
of a jacket.

NOW THAT I'VE MADE IT TO FLAVORTOWN, I JUST WANT TO GO HOME

Everything here is too spicy.
I'm tired of making a statement
every time I pick a restaurant.
There are no trophies
for most likes on a picture of ribs.
I miss going to whichever drive-thru
is on my way home. I miss
my uncle's burgers, so overgrilled
they turn into domes. I miss sitting
around a table and thinking
only about the friends across from me
instead of who can say "authentic"
first. When everyone at the table has to
go full Meg Ryan after every bite,
how can you even talk about anything?
Take me back to where a sandwich is free
to just be a sandwich.

S14E11: GUY FIERI'S DIVE & TACO JOINT, KANSAS CITY

EXT Power & Light, an *entertainment district* that is presumably "hoppin'" on weekend nights but on this cloudy and cold day is barren except for the line of people waiting to get into Guy Fieri's Dive & Taco Joint. POET is animatedly speaking to A PICTURE OF GUY FIERI on a sign.

> A PICTURE OF GUY FIERI
>
> ...

> POET
>
> Listen, the last thing I want to do is pull another Pete Wells. I think you're misunderstood. The people who make you a punching bag misunderstand you. The people who canonize you in that ironic, meme-y way misunderstand you. I am probably misunderstanding you right now. Pete Wells *definitely* misunderstands you. I think his review of your restaurant shone a light on the divide that was already there between the eating philosophy of privileged people in New York and the eating philosophy of people in the rest of the country. I'm glad people talked about it. I'm glad Marilyn Hagerty got famous reviewing that Olive Garden. I'm glad Tony gave her a book deal. I'm sad that the whole discussion needed you as a scapegoat. I love watching *Triple D*. I've often had great meals at places you highlight. I like that you use your platform to make small businesses busier. But bro, this new restaurant (sorry, joint) is not very good.

It seems like maybe you know it's not very good. Even though it's open, it's not listed on your website as one of your restaurants. Your voiceover in the promotional video goes, "you have gotta check out my new restaurant, killer cocktails, real deal food, and a rockin' good time, and I'll see you there." You never say the name of the joint, or even the city it's in. How many of your joints have posted the same promo video on their Facebook pages?

Plus, you and I both know I won't see you here. It's opening weekend and you're nowhere to be found. That means something. When a restaurant is filmed for *Triple D*, you spray paint a stencil on its walls that says "Guy ate here." Not "Guy endorses this food" or "Guy likes it here." "Guy ate here." Part of the attraction is the "here," your presence in a space as you eat the food.

RANDOM BYSTANDERS pause to watch POET yell at the sign. A few take out their phones to take videos for Snapchat. Unaware of them, POET continues, with rising intensity.

    POET
When you have a name and platform like yours, you can create entire worlds. You have the reach and the power to build Flavortown from the ground up. You've seen so much of the best food in this country. You know what's good. So when you find yourself in front of a blank canvas, this is what you come up with? A neon sign above the bar that says, "Namaste, bitches?"

I came here trying to like it. In this whole project I want to redeem you a bit, or at least to paint a more nuanced picture than "look at that affable goober with the sunglasses on his neck." I hope I can still do that without liking this restaurant, because this restaurant is bad. I ordered something called "Trash Can Nachos." Again, with all you've seen and eaten, the thing you think Americans want to eat is "Trash Can Nachos?" Or is that just what you think Americans will buy if your name is on it?

If you want details, the Trash Can Nachos were lukewarm and the chips were too soggy to lift any of the toppings. Some of the chips were just chip, which means your nacho/topping ratio is way off. A severely stoned sophomore at 2 a.m. could stumble upon the perfect chip/topping ratio. It's not rocket science.

The margarita was good, but for twelve bucks, can't you at least throw in a salt rim or a piece of fruit?

I'm responding cynically to your restaurant (sorry, joint) because the joint itself felt cynical. I know you know what good food is, and this is not good food. So why put your name on it? Surely it's not because tacos are a high-volume low-cost food that you can serve in a busy *entertainment district* to maximize your profit off of people who come here simply because they know your name is on the building? And here I thought Tony was supposed to be the cynical one.

My Trash Can Nachos spoke to me. They said, "Flavortown isn't a place, it's just another brand."

POET walks away, presumably back to his car to drive home. Unbe-
knownst to him, the garage where he parked is in the opposite direction.

.

LAST WILL & TESTAMENT

When I die, bury me at Randall Park Mall
beside the pebbled fountain where coiny water
once bubbled, by the stage where Tiffany sneakers
once danced and twirled. For the service, set out rows
of Brookstone massage chairs so the whir of the Shiatsu
hums as my Auntie Anne delivers a prayer through salty
tears. Let her introduce my eulogist, one of the KB Toys
Robot Dogs who will yip the story of me and backflip
as he barks "amen." Later, throw a party. Give the hordes
of mourners Orange Julius. Circulate among them waiters
in red aprons and silver trays who keep interrupting hilarious
Danny anecdotes to ask again if anyone wants to try
some chicken. Build my coffin of Legos and erect
a Playmobil train set atop my grave so children can play
God crashing trains as I watch from beneath the terrazzo.

ACKNOWLEDGEMENTS

"Guy Fieri Talks to Himself in his Trailer's Mirror before Going On Set" appeared in *Hobart*.

"Where Exactly is Flavortown, USA?" appeared in *The Harpoon Review*.

"The Flavortown Citizenship Test (With Trick Question)," "The Hotdogger's Wish," and "A Nickname for Every Dillons in Kansas Starting with the Four in Lawrence" appeared in *Sprung Formal* in altered form.

"All I Want for Christmas is All I Want for Christmas is You," "It's a Domino's Christmas," "It's a Holiday Inn Express Christmas" "It's a Cracker Barrel Christmas," and "It's a Waffle House Christmas" appeared in *Barrelhouse's Island of MisfitLit*, sometimes in altered form.

"The American Kidwest" appeared in *The New Territory* in altered form.

"Last Will & Testament," "Flavortown Gossip," and "Now that I've Made it to Flavortown I Just Want to Go Home" appeared in *Heavy Feather Review*.

"In the Bad Walmart's Parking Lot" appeared as a coaster at 715 Restaurant as part of The Coaster Poems Project, a collaboration of Raven Book Store, 715 Restaurant, and Blue Collar Press.

"The Wienermobile Sonnets" wouldn't exist without the book Dog Days: *A Year in the Oscar Mayer Wienermobile* by Dave Ihlenfeld. Also of invaluable assistance was an interview with my friend and former Hotdogger, Joe Besl.

Thank you to Gary and Harpoon Books for believing in this project and putting it out in such gorgeous form. Thank you to my friend and collaborator Tara Wray, whose photographs grace the covers of all my poetry books. Thanks to Kevin Cannon for his perfect work as Flavortown cartographer. Thank you to Hanif Abdurraqib, Chris Gonzalez, Daniel A. Hoyt, & Becky Mandelbaum for reading and supporting this manuscript early on. Thank you to PBR Writer's Club for helping me shape this book: Chance Dibben, Julia Gilmore Gaughan, Rachel McCarthy James, Maggie Bornholdt, Richard Noggle, Will Averill, and Althea Schnacke. Thanks to mom and dad and Matt for those nights watching *Triple D* on the couch. Thanks to Kara and Jack for the inspiration and support.

DANNY CAINE is the author of the poetry collections *Continental Breakfast* (Mason Jar Press 2019), *El Dorado Freddy's* (collaboration with Tara Wray, Belt Publishing 2020), and *Flavortown* (Harpoon Books, 2021) and the book *How to Resist Amazon and Why* (Microcosm Publishing, 2021). His poetry has appeared in *LitHub*, *DIAGRAM*, *Hobart*, and *Barrelhouse*, and his prose has appeared in *LitHub* and *Publishers Weekly*. The Midwest Independent Booksellers Association awarded him the 2019 Midwest Bookseller of the Year award. He lives in Lawrence, Kansas where he owns Raven Book Store.

CPSIA information can be obtained
at www.ICGtesting.com
Printed in the USA
FSHW021453130521
81329FS